Quatrains
& other short poems

Quatrains
& other short poems

Robert Notenboom

LEAKY BOOT PRESS

Quatrains & other short poem
by Robert Notenboom

ISBN: 978-1-909849-83-9

First published in 2019 by Leaky Boot Press
Copyright © 2019 Robert Notenboom

All rights reserved. This book, or any part thereof, may not be reproduced, stored in or introduced into a retrieval system, or transmitted, in any form or by any means, electronic, mechanical, photocopying, recording or otherwise, without the prior written permission of the publisher.

Quatrains
& other short poems

Inadvertently born and raised in France
I wrote in a tongue that was not mine
Now I've switched to a Saxon English
Searching for my poems the best shrine

Rats are clever animals
Who leave sinking boats
So do I, leaving a country
That doesn't love its poets

Words scribbled on my dreams...
As came the day
what I believed a poem
flew away

Sung is my song
Farewell! Cling, clang.
Does remain something
Of what I sang?

I've bought a diary for next year
What an act of faith!
Cautiously I chose black
Ready for my death

Look! this old man in front of you
So ugly and old has been a child
Dare stroke his wrinkled hands
Brotherly, silent, kind and mild

My bed is my raft
on a stormy ocean
sometimes it takes off
without any caution

I come from the dentist. now
I could anew bite with my teeth
but the tiger behind them is dead;
remains an old man of peace…

To keep them for myself alone
I softly locked the garden door
I aim to nothing else than roses
In this fleeting life and nothing more

In the courtyard of the hospital
Behind glass walls, a lonely tree –
My brother! With our branches and arms,
We greet each other hopelessly

Seldom going for a walk
I left well locked the garden gate
Having tea with Eva's snake. We chat
About time past   It's now so late

Today they cut me into slices
Of calf , of swine, of ham
How sad for whom dreamt to be an angel
Not to be more than I am

I love your laugh, your smile
The sparkle in your eyes
Don't listen to my words
Be happy in your lies

He wished his soul be clean and cleared
of bad thoughts, vanity and greed
It went light, light! and flew away
from him, at fullest speed.

I enter now the time of sadness
Sad are the words I still would write
Madness would be to darken your eyes
I love them so much bright open to light

Young, I failed to be a musician
Later, as a manager, I was rather bad
Therefore I flew to islands far off
Where poetry tries to live. How sad!

My only aim in life
Seems to survive! Odd
This funny ape who dreams
To be the son of God!

It was so comfortable not to publish
As during all her life did Emily
An angel came on my shoulder and said: "do it"
I did; t' was the end of my serenity

I don't write anymore.
What still you read from me,
are those pebbles I collected,
and left now on my way to sea

All those days spent
Lost or won?
What really matters
Is they're gone

I won't talk any more
Why add words to words?
I'll try to keep silent
As decided to do gods

As I don't travel any more
I pop from one to another tongue
It changes my way to think and see
Singing another song

I know, they're neither good nor bad
Don't be shy!
Although waiting for you, I'm not that sad
Ready to die

When she comes to take me off
I hope I'll keep me strong and steady
And say to her the battle was rough
OK, you won. Let's go. I'm ready

I love roses and butterflies
but also the pond and the sea
a rose, a bird, even the sky
all sharing the same fragility

From the east westwards
My boat will berth very soon
To birth or death
To sun or moon

I left the door half open
and savor quietly these noises
hasty footsteps muffled
laughs, tears, deadened voices

Shyly reddening
dying, flying leaves
believe
survive as butterflies

We met in times past
so young – love could not take root
that's what in any case
we believed

Jailed in myself
light dimmed
hearing muffled
beauty tries to clear its ways through night

Why did we meet as dusk is come?
God threw the dice
He shut his eyes,
He's the cat and we the mice

At early dawn
my boat has cast off
—now lost in mist

He said
I gave freedom to men and animals
to continents and seas
to planets and stars
and now I live an eternal and boring Sunday
I'll give now freedom to liberty
and retire You see
I'm a lazy god
Thus spoke the Lord
and fell asleep

There was a youngster
named Tomorrow
He wanted to go further
on working hard
and became a brilliant Yesterday
He never enjoyed being a Today

My bed is my boat
my dreams are my wings
I'm a happy bird

Be quiet, my heart
Listen in the mist of dusk
Noises of life, dimming

Sun warming my back
eyes closed to receive John Sebastian Bach
happy minutes stolen by time

Sunday
Day of the sun
As a son of the moon
I've chosen to slip away to sleep
Deep
Until comes my day
Brotherly bleak and blue

Trees are burning
their last leaves to gold
I savor my weary pace

It was a very strong beast
very long
with two heads
the first was a head of a crocodile
the other of a lamb
but as I said
the body of this beast was very long
really
and the crocodile's never could swallow the lamb's
and it was not the nature of the lamb to eat a
crocodile
so, they had to live together
each in his role
in the strange comedy of life

What could I say to ghosts hostile and foreign
When still unknown is who inspires my words?
How could I persuade those ghastly strangers?
And even if my language can be heard,
Remains that I to me is He to them.

Sometimes I overcome my days, imagining
A puppeteer pulling my strings and then
A hidden harmony is brought to light.

But cruel, that leaves no place to gleams,
Completed discourse reducing Mind to silence.

The deserted gardens of memory,
The silver coast I'll never reach,
The dreaming child along the beach
And the famous artist I couldn't be.

No more than a fugitive pain,
Like those twinges the years have brought,
I reduce myself to be a thought
Whose only joy is to remain.

When I die
forget my life
remember my dreams

Here was a flower
only remains now a scent
and laughing, the wind

Beside the tranquil pond,
the angler savors quietly
the softness of the ending day

In the basket at his feet
carps and pikes, stifling
are noiseless dying out

Waved by a light breeze,
trees are gently blessing
this holy scene of peace

Fallen sparrow
wings broken
I picked you up

I hold you in my hands
half closed
as would they be a nest
Doing my best
Not to hurt you

I felt you quiver
and beat your heart

I shyly dared stroke your feather
frightened
you looked at me
you saw a man
your bird catcher alike

I was so near to loving you
but your only wish was to fly away

Fearful ferrets
hidden in ferny fields
feverish dreamed of peace
freedom and love

Weird tigers and wolves
whispered fondly sweet words to them
and the hated world
fell down to nought

Lying is this always spring garden
as soon as leaves and flowers decease
gardeners replace them by others just born

My love
before we leave
just for a while
let us lie to ourselves
believe us eternal
eternal our love

Pacing some meters left
some meters right
up and down
I seldom see behind my wall
neither a flower, nor a tree

But dales between loose bricks
give life to dreams of meadows
jungle of dauntless weed
sometimes
majestic
a dandelion stands proud
and dares a wonder bloom
a sun
braving fate
teaching me late
that nothing's great and nothing's small

Read out my words
not too loud
just a whisper
then read them over
until ravenous ravens appear
and clear your souls of sated thoughts

Back to nought

Between Thebe's paving stones
flowers blossom in tiny dales
red and yellow

(After having heard 'The Seven Last Words
of Christ' by Joseph Haydn)

The day is over ; like me, the sun afar is bleeding.
My last words have been said. Let's go! You,
Who did not listen to me nor love me in truth,
Please, leave now the stage and let me alone!
No! there won't be at night the tempest foreseen;
Waves of sand will bury your derisory faith!
What happens? I'm waking up! Was it a dream?

There won't be many evenings like this
coffee drunk, dishes pushed aside and cigars lit
cheerful chats, heavy talks
eased in sparse mutterings

Night is come and time to wave goodbye

Let's walk along the shore
as many years ago we did
sharing days we lost

We met late in life
nearly ending is mine
yours woven with duties and dreams

Don't weep
how could I quench your thirst of love
quieten your sorrow
gently, yes, fondly, kill your hopes?

I'm no more a man
soon a ghost

Already lost

We're walking thoughtful along the shore
Listening, silences seldom shared

Behind the cliff, sun's now vanishing
As seagulls, immaculate, are landing

They write on the sand they take over
That time is come for us to leave

Treading upon fallen leaves
I see they've changed
to gold

Where did you bury the ancient child?
are you that sure he's dead?
maybe he's dreaming
screaming perhaps
in the depths of night

I'll go back to the Past
but the Past is Dead
OK! Death is my future

Now, I believe I leave very soon
Noisy streets and crowded places.
Taking an almost forgotten path
- views of it stream from my dream -
Shaded by fragrant and swaying pines,
Gently leading me back to sea.
In the coming dusk and dimming light,
Thousands of cicadas are cymbalizing,
Overwhelming the din of waves
So as not to scare me too much
As still I do pine for a last dawn.

Just before dying
he dressed up as a corpse

Young, he's been trained
to take in any circumstance
an appropriate demeanor

Strangled dreams
wrapped in a white towel
like kittens just born
born to die
thrown out
still hardly painfully breathing
trying to find an endless sleep
sweet and deep
empty of any hope

"Your boat, sir, is ready to sail"
For a short while he knew the last
His steps crunched sensuously
Gravel, pine needles and weed
On the path leading to sea.
Trees seem wave him good bye
Till he saw, hurrying him up
Quivering of hast, the mast.

I knew a world of fear and flight
I knew a world of hope
and light
now what remains is despair
and dope

Steel monster, cut me in slices
And tell me who masters my days
Which cells decided to rebel
I'm now like a king they dethrone
Little by little and cruelly kill

I was dreaming on a cloud
and heard a voice
"Go down, Bob
and start a new life!"
I did not answer and went back to sleep
that threat was a nightmare
Probably

"Which are your sins?"
asked He
none! was my answer
my old body does refuse!

Oh! I feel at my shoulder growing
wings!

You Soul
burdened with selfishness and greed
clung to ground
flies away

Does only remain
a small heap of ashes

For a long time I tried to love you
And perhaps in some way succeeded
I see in your eyes a promise of light
Few remain and come at my side

As I walk the way down to the shore
Nobody's holding my hand
as I board the small boat
motor humming, ready to put out to sea
Dark is the sky and rough the waves
Sleepy, smiling I don't quiver
and look at myself as already left

A hawk
from my shoulder suddenly
sprang
landing on my belly
shoved his cruel beak
on what made me a man
and whipped
and digged
and drilled
After a while
woozy
I awoke
"all is alright, sir"
said the nurse

Why do we shut the eyes to the dead?
Are we afraid
of what we could see of ourselves?
what do we dread?
hearts dried out
hopes drooping slowly?

Why
Do we want so hasty to escape,
shunning this peace unknown
to dive into a world of noise and fury
to which we've been tamed

However, so peaceful is the corpse
left by a last breath
flown away to the sky

I let my paces find the way
As dreams had sowed in them my aim
That blooms and birds made me forget

But I was tired and tired the day
A look to trees vanished in dusk
A thought to you, before I pray

to hear the noises of days
deadened voices, footsteps
muffled, fears and joys
Vaguely, smiling to life.

www.ingramcontent.com/pod-product-compliance
Lightning Source LLC
LaVergne TN
LVHW041549070426
835507LV00011B/1014